BLOOD

THIRSTY

SAVAGES

BLOOD THIRSTY SAVAGES

POEMS BY

Adrian C. Louis

TIME BEING BOOKS®
POETRY IN SIGHT AND SOUND

Time Being Books®
10411 Clayton Road
St. Louis, Missouri 63131

Time Being Books® volumes are printed on acid-free paper, and binding materials are chosen for strength and durability.

Time Being Books® is an imprint of Time Being Press, Inc.
St. Louis, Missouri

ISBN 1-56809-010-2
ISBN 1-56809-011-0   (pbk)

Library of Congress Cataloging-in-Publication Data:

Louis, Adrian C.
    Blood thirsty savages : poems / by Adrian C. Louis.
        p.   cm.
    ISBN 1-56809-010-2 (hc) — ISBN 1-56809-011-0 (pb)
    1. Indians of North America — Poetry.   I. Title.
    PS3562.082B55   1994
    811'.54—dc20   94-7444
                                                               C I P

Cover painting by Don Montileaux
Book design and typesetting by Lori Loesche
Manufactured in the United States of America

First Edition, first printing (July 1994)

Acknowledgments

Some of these poems, a few in earlier versions, have appeared in periodicals including *Ploughshares*, *TriQuarterly*, *The Chicago Review*, *Chelsea*, *Aura*, *North Dakota Quarterly*, *New Virginia Review*, *Caliban*, *Agassiz Review*, *Contact II*, *Exquisite Corpse*, *Red Dirt*, *Zeitgeist*, *Prairie Winds*, *The Hawaii Pacific Review*, *The Heartlands Today*, *Cream City Review*, *The Clouds Threw This Light*, *Pemmican*, *The Antioch Review*, *Blank Gun Silencer*, *Poetry Motel*, *The Chiron Review*, *Blue Mesa Review*, and *The Howling Mantra*. Grateful acknowledgment is made to the editors of these publications.

Thanks to fellowships from the Bush Foundation and the National Endowment for the Arts, I was allowed the time to compose many of these poems. Moreover, once in the middle of high plains winter when I was almost down for the count, there were anonymous angels who came to my aid. You know who you are. I was too ill to know exactly how many of you danced on the head of my pin, but I thank each one of you. *Aho*. Last, but not least, I'd like to express my gratitude to Hayden Carruth.

For Jeanne
who lives in my heart
and for Colleen
who lives in my house.

These poems are dedicated
to those friends
who have come
and gone
like a prairie hailstorm
only to reappear
in the penitentiary
or on the obituary pages.

Many days you have lingered
all around my cabin door.
Oh hard times,
come again no more!

Contents

BLOOD THIRSTY SAVAGES

We had buffalo for food,
and their hides
for clothing and our tipis.
We preferred
hunting to a life of idleness
on reservations where
we were driven against our will.

At times
we did not get enough to eat, and
we were not allowed to leave
the reservation to hunt.
We preferred our own way of living.
We were no expense to
the government then.
All we wanted was peace
and to be left alone.

—Tasunke Witko (Crazy Horse)

Part One

VARIED PRAYERS

A Prayer for the Lost

for Marilyn Nelson Waniek

To escape marauding in-laws
whose kids slosh Kool-Aid
against the walls of my heart
and moisten the dry-dirt memories
of my own childhood,
I slink outside carrying garbage
in two green plastic sacks
and armor them in steel drums
to baffle the blood-eyed pack
of coyotes that nightly sneaks
up from the creek.

The laundered April air
and the effervescent stars
make me forget for a moment that life
as I know it is dying and I think
I might live forever among the wild-ass Sioux.

In a neighboring house, a dope dealer's wife
holds a brown baby sprouting
from her cantaloupe breasts.
An enabling moon is rising and clattering cars
racket and rupture any dreams of true love.
In the purity of starlight, I ask Grandfather
to salvage this battered Indian nation
because my words may be no help.
Should the coyotes burst the cold
steel drums, pale white flowers would bloom.
Upon countless crumpled pages
variants of this prayer for the lost
would be found.

A Post Card from Devils Tower

TEXAS TRAIL 1866-1897
Along This Trail Passed Herds Of Cattle
From Distant Texas
To Replace The Fast Vanishing Buffalo
And Build A Civilization
On The North Western Plains
— Words on a granite marker
at Moorcroft, Wyoming

Send the buffalo hunters powder and lead, if you will,
but for the sake of lasting peace, let them kill, and
sell, until the buffalos are exterminated. Then your
prairie can be covered with the speckled cattle, and
the festive cowboy, who follows the hunter as the
second forerunner of advanced civilization.
— General Philip Sheridan
(in an 1873 address to the Texas Legislature)

I.

Brothers, I am the truth, sometimes glazed
but always the truth.
Crazy Horse drove this same highway
at times so weary with his people
that he pretended to go *hanbleceya*
but instead put on old white man clothes
and worked the intruders' ranches
cutting hay and branding cattle
and bunking with the rest
of the hired hands.

Sometimes we must lie to survive
and in this heinous lie I do live.
Zipping past Rapid Creek in the vicinity
of where Crazy Horse was born, I
heard the radio say a severe thunderstorm
would slap the Black Hills tonight.
Coming into Rapid City, I smelled
the new cut hay which gave way
to the stench of the sewage plant.

Maybe I might stay in town tonight.
I never told her where I was headed.
Just said I'm going and she said, "So go."
My grudging march is acceptable escape.
This self-enforced vacation from each other
found me driving north from Pine Ridge
through the Badlands, past Scenic,
into the Paris of the Plains.
Damn. Crazy Horse had to have
driven this same world.

II.

Rapid City, the height of the tourist season.
After two hours of cruising I find
a motel with a reasonable rate,
sputtering air conditioner and greasy floor rugs.
Sleep is short-circuited. Dreams come quickly
and briefly, unremembered like
commercials in a boxing match.
At six in the morning the car heads for McDonald's.
At seven it takes off for Mt. Rushmore.
After eight years in this state
I figure I'll view the horror that I've
held in contempt for most of my life:
those massive stone idols of Indian killers.
This is one nation under God
but there is no escaping *those* demons.
Sometimes they come
in a gust of jest—
their toothless smiling faces pressed against
the glass of passing cars
and sometimes their eyes reflect the stars
but mostly they just bleed murder.
Halfway to the stone fools,
the car turns back to Rapid.

III.

In unfettered air, crystal sunshine
halos my car gliding North on I-90
past Lead and then past Deadwood.
This town where Wild Bill Hickock
bought the farm is not much more than
a miniscule festering scab
imitating Las Vegas with casinos,
nondescript whores and eternal tackiness.
The intruders' diseases plague these sacred hills.
The car zips past Sturgis where already biker
trash are congregating like flies
on the dead balls of America.
Getting gas in Spearfish, I blink at the map
and decide to drive to Devils Tower,
another place I've never seen, not out of
contempt but because it's tourist flypaper.
At nine, the car pulls into Sundance, Wyoming
and my flesh enters a Conoco Mini-Mart.
Strangely, it is filled with Indians
from Pine Ridge, there for the Sacred Hoop
Five Hundred Mile Run, a yearly event.
The skins seem miscast, slightly downcast
in the brightness of the small white town.
We toss a few hellos back and forth
and the car is off on the twenty mile road
that snakes to the Tower.

IV.

The first sight of the Tower ten miles away
is like a slap in the face.
The closer I get, the more I imagine
the wry smile on the Creator's face
when he manufactured it.

Finally reaching the ranger station
at the base, words cringe

and refuse to seek air.
The Tower assaults my soul.
Nothing has prepared me for this.
This is the eternal cathedral
of the Great Spirit.
Were I to awake one morning and find
the prize between my thighs
had doubled in length
I would have been less impressed
than this first visit to the Tower
but brothers, the Government owns it.
The Government owns it,
just like it owns our Indian asses.

Sifting the Ashes of Greek Fire

> *. . . the dark pulse of her scum turning*
> *gold in a perfection only the absolute*
> *correction of lust can know.*
>
> — Joe Cardillo

The eyes have it
or so you said
and words were pastiched,
tumbled into waters
that should have dried
upon the dong but did not.
Aliki, the howling curs
had collars of gold.
The only word
they knew was
love.

Your music of life held
whispers of the Ark.
My dark scrawl of survival,
my twisted footprints of history
declined the voice.
The way I heard it,
the white boys
at the gas station
were always pumping Ethel.
So what was that liquid you sold?
The lakes of hell flamed
with sound, not sight.
The bubbling of blood,
the harsh crackling
of flesh was exquisite.
My boiling eyes drooled
in their sockets
but those very eyes had had it.
I told you to tell Homer I wanted
to go home and rhyme
my lifeline with forty-nine.
That last night twelve years ago

when you tied me against the dark,
I awoke and wandered
to the kitchen where you found
me and called me "survivor"
and said I looked like Odysseus
downing a can of Bud.
The cool liquid trickled
down to my fiery crotch
and tricked me into silence.
We were both naked but unaware.
Thick books of criticism
were stacked everywhere.
They blocked any vision of skin.
Resumed or re-doomed,
the words we coined
could not pay the fare of such folly.
We vowed to never be dead
and not read.
In your spacious scrawl
your words made you dance
erotically beyond the control of age.
At mid-life, you were an impish child,
a dervish dressed in Grecian clouds,
and you danced
quite madly on Ithaca's shore.
You said your past
was not part of my dream.
God knows I did not
share mine with you.
From commodities to outhouses,
from drum to wine,
it was mine, my mind.
Darling, the fool that I was would
have never stood before the naked
and boisterous world boasting:
I am Odysseus,
son of Laertes.

All men take account
of my wiles
and my fame
has reached high heaven.
My home is in Ithaca,
fair in the evening light.

I only said I was a half-breed Paiute
Indian lost in the melodrama
of our love and longing for the sage
covered hills of my homelands.

And I would not say
that we were incandescent
though distantly decent, the cant
in which we writhed and wrote
and lied illuminated
was nothing more than a bulb
with a fractured element flickering.
Aliki, our lamplight was darkening.
Something was sure as hell broken
inside the vacuum in which we loved.
It was not agoraphobia.
Our marketplace transcended sight.
And no, you were not Aphrodite
or even Penelope.
At 2 a.m. that night twelve years ago
when you called us quits
and screamed for me to get out
of your house,
I said nothing
as I packed my bags.

Nothing seemed fair to me
because America has never
been fair to Indian people.
In your white words I heard
the ghostly scurrying

of immigrant hordes
and the death songs
of many red nations.
I stole a pair of your panties
to remember you by.
They were red.
Sweet Jesus, they were bright red
and they followed me
back here to Indian land.
Someday, someday I will send them back
when their static electricity quits
zapping my face.

Last Song of the Dove

During the second week of jets
dive-bombing Iraq on CNN,
Jake Red Horse said he stumbled
to shave the face of a middle-aged drunk
whose boyhood contempt of America
had eroded, cracked, and fallen away
like an old man's teeth.
His evil twin smiled back at him
from the bathroom mirror.
He washed his dentures and injected
them into his wordless mouth.
When he returned from the toilet,
Vice-President Quayle was sound-bitten
saying comforting, cheerleading war words
to a group of flag-waving yahoos.
They fell for him, hook, line, and sinker
and so did Jake's evil double.

In those weeks before Americans
wearied of widespread massacre,
Jake's Doppelgänger relished burned tanks
and charred bodies with pure delight.
He had wet dreams for the dark sex of war.
Just because the President had jumpstarted
a crusade against the peoples of Allah
didn't mean his evil twin had any peace
in his heart left over from the sixties.
Both waved the flag in their own warped way
while they silently prayed for an end to the war
which came shameful and heartless
in the folly of victory.
It was televised, grandly choreographed
and swarmed with invisible maggots.
Six weeks later it was all but forgotten.

Verdell's Morning Constitutional

Somebody's left-out cat was screaming
at the ghosts of summer larks.
It was twenty-God-damn-seven
below out and the air hurt to breathe, but
Verdell Ten Bears took his morning constitutional.
Under the colorless sky, he wobbled
towards the bootlegger's for a pint of whiskey
and for one brief second in his snow-toed trek
he winced at the queerness of his icebox world
before the shimmering d.t.'s hit him.

A flock of bug-eyed, naked angels
minced around and blocked his path.
They asked ugly and intrusive questions
just like goofy Phil Donahue.
Verdell plugged his ears and kept on trudging.

The naked angels danced lewdly
along his path like fire ants were marching
through and thawing their frozen veins.
They did the weirdest, butt-shaking
Hammer dance, oomphing down the chilled road
running alongside Verdell's shadow
with foam icicles forming at their mouths.
They were prickteasing the tired reservation
with sweet whispers of springtime.
Verdell knew what was happening.
He shrugged, smiled, and outdanced the angels
who grew ashamed and winged their sad souls
home to the Sky God's condo.

Another Indian Murder

Beneath Mt. Rushmore's
heightened air, drunk redskins
were stumbling everywhere
dead but for the deed of dying.
Inside crossed ruins around the town
pallid priests in rich robes lounged
sucking the lobes and loins
of a God they were sure
could never have fathered such action.

Their rosaries can't lighten
the darkness at will
so prone before Jesus
and white history's swill,
I prayed that the Sioux become sober
and quit murdering themselves, their great nation.

But, that bitter December night, the granite shadows
of Lincoln and Washington descended the slopes
and infected all that was good below.
Two Oglala boys with baseball bats
scrambled the brains of a drinking buddy
and when they sobered
they could not recall
how they tried to plug the brain-seeping
holes with Kleenex while they prayed
to the Lord to let him live.

For My Lakota Woman

Early that winter we had fresh tomatoes.
Whole plants yanked up by their roots
hung upside down in our basement.
Once rock hard and green, the globes
were slowly ripening.
My woman sent me down to pick one.
Trying hard to please after days
of being a bastard, I jogged back up
carrying the red fruit like a faithful
dog pleasing its master.
She calculated then rubbed
the tomato to my face
whetting my boyish charm
while her other arm
flashed a knife and
like a textbook wife
she sliced my brain between
the lettuce and tomato.
I caressed the stained enamel
of the kitchen sink
and strained for pleasant conversation.
On the counter tomato juice
had dried into Rorschach:
a pallid rose of my own weakened blood.
In the housing unit down the road
a white-haired *unci*, blanket bundled
against winter, was emptying the air
of frozen diapers upon a line.

Jesus Christ on a totem pole!
This was the hundred year
anniversary of Wounded Knee
and our lives flickered briefly
in televised soundbites
the Americans had written for us.

Part Two

VAGRANT COUSINS

Dreaming of Deer Woman

Outside, garlands of snow glistened
the brows of foraging field mice
in the full moon of owls.
They scampered to scour something
from nothing though it was in my power
to make frybread on woodstove I wouldn't.
I knelt, blessed them through the sights
of my air rifle and fed them lead.
I made a feast for a convocation
of feral Indian cats. I got hungry myself
watching their claws auger flesh.

The saber-slashing troopers have shape-shifted
into triglycerides, cholesterol, and carcinogens,
but this government is still killing us . . .

I clicked off the Indian radio station, opened
the can of USDA commodity stew
and shoveled down the lardish concoction.
That year I was trapped between screaming
stomach thoughts and the groin's need
for subhuman touch.
A middle-aged drunk still into Led Zep,
I'd been shown the way so many times
that I'd forgotten that romance was rotten
so sometimes my ghost would be up
at the high school with decades of dropouts
cruising the campus at lunchtime.

I shoveled down the federal lard stew
and danced an illusion homeward
through legions of sagebrush and piñon pine.
My eternal lie was that someday I'd sit
on the earth and stoke the campfire with
a pregnant brown woman busy humming
and cooking me wild-tasting deer flesh.

Spirit-Deer Deep in Pine Forests

The bad parts of Los Angeles are self-infected
with drugs, murder, and laziness
of mood, music, spirit.
Little wonder the riots occurred.
The safe parts of the city are homesteaded
by those who lobotomize America
though movies and television.
The city bus is a shaking sardine
can of crackheads and derelicts
with souls as scarred as the sands of Somalia.
An article in the *Times* notes huge mudslides
in the hills surrounding the city.
Like liquid croquet mallets, rains knocked
mountains of mud upon the homes of the rich
making them all as brown as the Dakota
plains where my small house stands
and for a moment I am faintly amused
by God's loose bowels
brown-shirting Babylon.

When I exit the bus at the university
where they're paying me
to enhance with safe distant words
the romance they think they see
inside my whirling soul's poverty,
I can't help but wonder how
much better off I'd really be
if I were a quadruple amputee or
a spirit-deer
fucking deep
in pine forests.

Verdell: Two Soliloquies

I.

Looking rougher last winter,
my *kola* Verdell Ten Bears
with face booze-sheened
and dirt-stiff jeans announced
he had fallen off the wagon again
and hit me up for a loan.
Hours later he came back, asked for more.
He wasn't asked why he was on this binge
but Verdell felt compelled to speak:

"I was born and died.
Hahh. Forget the rest
except for this scar on my chest.
In 'Nam something gushed from me there,
this creature that slithers and stinks
and breaks through walls
on wondrous tragic nights like this
when I am broke and needing wine
to quiet that medevac chopper."

II.

Later, after I paid
for his medicine, he said this:

"One time I went stoned out and greasy
to the Pine Ridge *wacipi*
and stood next to these *wasicu*
with cameras timidly taking
pictures of us dancing skins.
I strutted up to this skinny white woman
and smiled so damn hard she smiled back.
Then I got the dry heaves
and she headed out quick
with her bony butt bouncing
away from my retching.
Ennut, I think I coulda had her
if my stomach behaved
but God's goosing me
without grease these days."

Reclaiming an Old Debt

Our discussion of pleasures
of the text withered when I juxtaposed
Jocasta and *jouissance* in the same sentence.
So what if your twenty-year-old son
was sleeping in the next room?
I thought I'd planted closure when I stood
and let my hothouse hands
vine up your querulous thighs
and bring the balm of retrieved wetness
to the desert of my lips.
After that, you refused to tell me to leave.
The giggles of fate goosed my green bones.
I did push-ins to make the sweetest songs.
Years later, when my first wrinkles formed
your memory was then re-tooled.

You made me get lost in that eternal
search for flesh forgotten.
I should have trudged up the foetid, brown ditch
that was writhing with death snakes
instead of giggling nervously and tiptoeing
to the dancing brook where I bit
the heads off singing sprites.

What choice was there between clichés?
I would not have slow-syrup lack of breath
from a mouthful of clay and ribs
nor head-bashing heart-taking stone.
There were no rapids coursing to the sea,
no salt of tears and no Eurydice, so dear,
dear lady, can I have back my heart?

Fullblood Girl on a Blue Horse

for Luis Rodriguez

I don't know
why I sobered up and moved
from the rez down the road
twenty miles to this cow town.
The rednecks across the street
are partying and I am trying
to mow my weedy lawn.
One cowpoke chucks a beer
bottle and it explodes
on the street bordering
the back edge of my yard.
This Nebraska town
(Population: 1,492)
is a dried-up cowturd.
The only thing that keeps
it from blowing away
is the money the Indians
bring to town and yet
the greatest redneck joy is
hating and baiting Indians
and trying to keep us down.

Another bottle shatters . . .
I want to go get my pistol
and make that heifer-humper
crawl up the street
and pick up the glass shards
with his teeth and tongue.
My blood pressure is rising.
I want to make him cry
and piss his pants, but
I simply shut off the old mower
and shuffle down to the Post Office.
Maybe their party will be done
by the time I get back.
Maybe Wovoka's dream will

finally come true and all
the white folks will vanish.
Might as well hope it will snow
in July or the Pope will shoot
a commercial for condoms
and dildos and such.

This mailbox outside the Post Office
on Main Street is my thought temple.
It stands alone in defiance
of nature and winos.
Like a fortress of solitude
or a holy shrine,
it's a steel blue altar
for scrawled secrets of mine.
Those sacred words
I place inside
are useless bits
of wounded pride
and more that matters
even less but today
something is amiss.
A beautiful girl straddles
the mailbox.

Definitely high on something
this long-legged fullblood
girl with teenaged thighs
sits astride the cold blue
box like it is a wild stallion flying
her over this prairie town and
stampeding my once-green heart.
She smiles at me when I open
the chute and slowly insert
my letters and bills.
Grandfather! For one brief
moment of pained delight
electricity snaps in my pants.

Then I turn and strut
proudly towards home
but halfway there
I feel old and tired
and I pray I don't shoot me
some rednecks today.

Tangled Up in Lilac

for Patrick Stanhope

In the dusk of my dog-ruined backyard
I suck in the pungent spring air.
Tangled up in lilac, my yellow kitten stalks
a butterfly breaking curfew.
I watch her for a while and then move
on to larger thoughts of lust and liquor.
When I first went to bars, it wasn't for women
or booze, but for keys to the secrets
of this spinning dirt clod.

When I first started smoking, I did so
to look older but this is no list
of my vices and their derivations.
This is only a prayer for black, dreamless sleep.
The moon leers through my tallest cedars
and darkness extends its claws
and shreds any clarity of thought.
This sobriety does not come in sweet softness
but in the mechanical clutches of remembered desires.
My clenched and empty fists are still haunted
by ten thousand ghost bourbon bottles.
Maybe I am as strong as I ever have been.
Maybe I am as weak as my drunken neighbors
fighting and puking, chaotic and angry,
in the invisible *stalag* their minds
have designed.

A Brand New Snag

Above the budding cottonwoods
low flying clouds
pregnant with anger
barge the frozen earth
along the river of blackness.
On Sunday, the little brother
of Verdell's wife dies
from complications of diabetes.
On Tuesday, the elderly father
of Verdell's girlfriend journeys
to the spirit world with cancer.
Thursday, Verdell gets chest pains
from being pulled too hard
in two distinct directions
and is ambulanced to the V.A.
up in Hot Springs.
Tests show his heart is strong.
Reduce stress, the doctors say.
Friday, he falls off the wagon
he's been riding for four months
and ends up drinking
with a brand-new snag.
A young one.
A young one with tight braids.
Firm, still growing titties.

Notes on the New Dark Ages

I.

The poetry scholar visits the AIDS patients
and carries home their latest poems.
It is Halloween and they'll soon be ghosts.
She becomes a jack-o-lantern.
False smile carved with temporal light
her candled eyes join bats in flight.
She swallows their viral suffering
because she will profit.
She is hollow and yellow
and *such* an American but she
scares me because she can't scar.

II.

This same lady poet can only write what she reads!
But then what do we know?
Just last week I was driving,
thinking about the Nazi Goebbels
and the destruction of decadent German art
when my T-Bird jumped a curb
and careened down an alleyway
chasing a wino who looked like Dylan:
the master "poet" of my graying generation.

Ghosts Dance Among the Pine Trees Outside the Kmart

He was drunk, looked really pissed off
and I knew he must be close to broke
because the week before he borrowed ten from me.
Sitting in his battered '69 Chevy stinkbomb,
with wife and six kids quiet with fear,
one of my students named Samuel
sucked down a quick pint of wine.
Outside, imported pine trees
wooed the passers-by and pitched
the need to buy objects.

"Yeah, we're going to buy an Xmas tree
and stick it up fat Santa's butt!"
I heard him yell at his old lady
outside the Kmart in Rapid City.
"Get us a gallon of Vaseline."

I turned invisible and walked past, pretending
not to see in his explosion of misery
the dark ghosts of my own
Indian childhood
still dancing angrily
among the trees.

The Heart Is Also Flesh

When you say you love me
and cuddle my cock,
I don't mean to confuse you by blurting,
"The heart is also flesh."
My soul's been tainted by education
but I am like many men you know.
When I was rock-fist tough
and wet-dream young,
my mind was margarine soft.
I would have ruined you back then.
My heart was not flesh but bone.

Now, after our dance between
the decades of your Rosary
and in the sweet spring forest
of your primeval nakedness,
I pray that it is the warrior
spirits of my ancestors
and not the spurt of my lust
that defines you, my darling.
I love you and I'm very troubled.

What the hell will we name our son?

Sonnenkinder

Sober for four years I felt it
safe to make a whiskey run for Verdell.
Slowed by a luminous legion of farmers
driving home from parched fields
my T-Bird sputtered
through the eye-filled night
wheezing from point A to pointless.
Evening madness in the Middle West:
shadowed amber waves of grain
flat land corn, flat lack of rain,
the awkward shadows of flat human pain.
This is the glut of America . . .
This is our white bread basket . . .

Stopping in Gordon, Nebraska
for a fifth of Old Crow, I bumped into
one of the reservation priests
buying a case of expensive scotch
but I averted my ears from slurred sanctimony.
Christ, who in their half-right mind
would want to wrestle a zealous scarecrow
stuffed to muscularity with a dozen varieties
of righteousness—all Biblical and constipated?
The steel trap of his Jesuit mind
had completely rusted shut.
In his stupor he sidled up, spittle
at the corner of his mouth
and asked for a light.
Flapping my wings I tossed a match
and broke into dizzying flight.
I am a child of the sun
and moonfire can't touch my air.
I am a child of the sun
and brimstone can't touch my heart.

And yes, it's a bitter lie when I say I'm glad
I can never drink whiskey again.

Jake's Assessment of Last Winter

Light leaks into my life.
Some call it sobriety.
I know it's not silver.
      — Rane Arroyo

His right hand held the pulse
of instinct as natural as droning bees
while his left hand spasmed
computerized pleas.
Any attempted balance
between the two
was so incomprehensible
to him that he fell
to his sober knees and prayed
but Jesus was AWOL that winter day
when Jake wearied of drinking
and turned inward
and hiked up the hill
to the brain tune-up clinic.

Because he was sinking fast
he let a latter day
Viennese sausage priest
with a cheap M.A.
from a piss-poor school
trephine the lodestones in his mind
and remind him to try to be kind
as he pocketed his emerald days
and openly scoffed
at his Indian ways, at *our*
quickly diminishing Indian ways.

Part Three

THE BLOOD THIRST OF VERDELL TEN BEARS

The Blood Thirst of Verdell Ten Bears

One.

In the beginning there's only a hint of dangerous things to come. My name is Verdell Ten Bears & I'm planning to kill me a man in Pine Ridge. How come us Indians are forever falling down the toilet to Hell? Why do I keep putting my middle-aged boy body in dangerous situations? I always ask "why," hoping that by poking my finger into the eye of pain, pain will be chickenshit & run & healing will come, but *ennut,* that never does happen. I go on stepping in the same pile of crap, winter after winter, woman after woman. I'm not retarded & I'm not a slow learner. I'm forty-two years old & dashing through the gray stadium of South Dakota winter like a sex-crazed rabbit. I'm clutching her welfare check in my grubby, shaking paw & I've endorsed her name on it. I need the money & I'm doing a hobbling dash through sanded snow as fast as I can but I move like a retarded elephant with fire ants biting his balls. This is what happpens when you drink hard twenty years. I crash through the cruddy clumps of snow to get to the Rapid City Bus Depot. Running is not my solution to the riddle of the universe. Each step is a "why." Each gasp pains lung air & no answer comes. I've got some money & I'm going back home to the rez. Why? Why must I ask? For reals, I'm planning to kill me a man in Pine Ridge.

Two.

I dribble my lonely blubber towards the bus & think
of my loony heart. Walk, wiggle, stop, shake, walk.
I might look like a purse snatcher on the run but I
ain't a crook. Stick a needle in my eye & damn hope
to die. I used to be a pipeline welder. Laid a lot of
pipe. I'm a Viet vet. Heck yes, I forged her check but
Christ, we been living together for five years. The
check was only for two hundred bucks & she'd just
drink it up anyways. She must know I gotta return to
the rez. It was her who threw me out. Tossed me out
like a used condom. Her & her college ways. She
even has a book on Moby Dick the whale. Jesus, I
never knew nobody who had a book on Moby Dick.
She made me try twice to read it but it was too hard
& didn't make no sense. She said it related to us
Indians but I don't see how. She thinks my brain is
half-toasted & yet she claims to love me. She won't
after she sees her missing check. So what? I went to
the tribal community college for two years. She ain't
the only educated one. At least I don't have a book
on Moby. She never even liked the jokes I made on
Moby's last name. Well, screw her & the whale she
rode in on. I've gotta go kill me this dude.

Three.

I shimmer across the icewalk & just miss sliding into a Rapid City cop. She's a white whale, a bigfat Dickless Tracy. She gives me a fish-eye look & I look back at her gun & keep on shuffling down the road. She yells something at my back but I keep going. In the crisp air I have a vision of starving eagles. Hah! This is a weird movie! In the corner of my eye, they flock. Dozens of the huge birds looping the loop. They are man-sized & have razor claws. They could rip a damn whale to shreds. One hushed swoop & the land could be ribboned with meat, puddled with blood. All for a lousy two hundred bucks I stole. I'm getting paranoid. I imagine cars that follow me down the sidewalk, turning my footprints in the snow into a hundred faces of the man I'm going to kill. The face of death won't be so handsome. Death is a scraggly drag queen with smeared lipstick. How does a bullet feel? It slants silent in descent & then it rapes the flesh. I know. I been shot. But now I'm a little scared. Fat me, two hundred & twenty-six pounds, sweating, panting, my scrotum shriveling, my eyes stinging, I run like a morphadyke goofball to the bus depot. I'm carrying a stolen check & I'm going to buy me a gun.

Four.

Strange how everything goes without a hitch & I cash
her welfare check. They take it with no questions at
the Indian bar by the bus depot so I have a quick shot
of Jack Daniels & two bottles of Bud. I even buy a
round for two rum-dumb winos from Rosebud & get
me a pint of Jack Daniels to go. At the OK Pawn
Shop I buy a .22 Llama pistol & a box of long rifle
shells for sixty bucks. It's a cheap little gun for a
cheap little life. Then, at Woolworth's I buy a
package of three Fruit of the Looms. Don't want to
be walking around in smelly shorts. I put it all in a
big paper sack & walk to the waiting bus & climb in.
It takes off like a whining dog & looks like a fat silver
whale. Smells like Lysol mixed with puke & pizza.
Down inside the cave of the paper bag, the small
pistol is shining black. It's the real damn thing. I try
to close my eyes & sleep. The bus groans south
towards the dead man who waits. A woman behind
me is whispering in Indian to a small child with a
pee-smell diaper. The kid lets out a storm of big
screams. His mother clucks, his mother coos. The
kid quits his crying & I start mine. My tears are
inside the paper bag inside the plastic bag. My tears
are sloshing inside the pint bottle of Jack.

Five.

Bitter bile is snaking up my gut towards my voiceless throat. I'm getting seasick on this whale bus. I don't need Dramamine, but I wish I had the guts of guys like the astronauts. Those were the real heros of this dying nation. They left the home fires of earth & put their asses on the line. Who knows? There could be slime-dicked geeks up there in outer space whose only reason for living is to stick steel scalpel tongues into human brains. I've seen mutilated cattle in the Badlands, teats & ears cut off. There could be anything up there, even God, God forbid. Astronauts gotta have balls of brass. Or maybe they had no balls at all. That'd explain their non-fear of death. I wish I had courage instead of pimples on the brain. The winter sun is dancing against the bus windows & everything. This old world is golden & pure. I wish I wasn't hanging over. This morning I took three Tylenol, a pot of black coffee, a hot & cold shower & a double shot of vodka. This shaking bus is going to make me puke & I'm sitting here thinking of asswipe astronauts. I'm burying my worries with thoughts of no meaning.

Six.

I couldn't blame her if she called the cops on me
though she never would.   I wouldn't blame her for
hating me. She's gotta watch out for her ownself &
our kids first. I ain't had a steady job in years, but I'm
grateful she's been supporting us for *dona* years on
AFDC & welfare checks. She's good that way. I
remember she was sitting on a bench in the park by
the creek in Rapid City by the bronze Indian statue
when I met her. I was drinking "Green Lizard" &
watching girls go by & she was looking good six
years ago but now she's as big as me. I took her to the
Oasis Bar & let her have her way with my ear for
several beers & then we went back to the creek. In
the bushes, not far from some winos sleeping it off,
we did it in the dirt just like dogs. Now here I am
carrying a paper bag holding a .22 pistol. It's black
& shiny & makes me feel ignorant, I smile when I get
off the bus in Rushville & stroll towards the edge of
that redneck Nebraska town. I stick out my thumb &
the golden sun falls behind the pine hills. Twenty
cars pass me before some tuned-up skins pick me up
& swerve me towards the South Dakota state line.

Seven.

Riding in the fartsack Indian car to Pine Ridge Rez, I think of her. Sometimes I used to feel like she'd completely blended her mind with me like Spock's Vulcan mindprobe on "Star Trek." The *tahansis* in the car offer me some bad wine which I taste to be hospitable. Their sacramental bottle touches soon-to-be-dead lips again & again. *I think of how she made me get a cot in the basement of our small house in Rapid. I quit sleeping with her. She knew I didn't like fat women. Drunk once, she said if I had to pick up some women, at least I'd have a place to bring them. Who are you, my mother, I asked & then went out to a bar to see if I really could. I couldn't & came home late to find her in bed, cuddled up with a half eaten pizza & a box of Whitman chocolates. Herds of beer cans surrounded the bed like all those little candles in Catholic Church. I laid next to her & while she snored, I did myself off.* Two guys in the front seat are arguing & then the driver slams on the brake & the two fools are out on the farmland highway duking it out. I tighten my grip on the bag holding my gun. Screw those guys, the driver says & peels out leaving their swing-banging knuckles behind him. We pass through White Clay & then hit Pine Ridge. He drops me at the Conoco station & I go in & get a cup of sixty-cent coffee.

Eight.

Outside the Conoco, two boys are fist-fighting. How can a man live a decent life? When I see white clouds dance past the moon in the black night, I think of murder. When I see black crows dancing on the fleshy ribcage of a road-killed deer, I think of snow. There is always the battle of lightness & darkness. This is the curse of my people. I could never put my nose to the grindstone. I stayed with my grandmother when I was growing up. She had a grindstone. We used it for sharpening knives & the axe. The axe was for killing chickens. I found that if you catch a chicken & draw a line in the dirt in front of it, it will become paralyzed. If you draw an invisible line, the damn same thing will happen. Bend their head down & draw the line. They cannot move. Do this on an old tree stump & then you whack off their heads. But once their brain is gone, they wake up & do a wild, blood dance. If you hypnotize two young cocks & make them face each other, they'll do a stare-down for a long time & when they finally come to, they will fight. Just like the two boys outside are doing. Just like I am doing with myself.

Nine.

Another time drunk I tiptoed into the house & peeked at her in our whale-sized bed. She was asleep crossways on the bed & it woulda took a D-9 Caterpillar to move her snoring flesh. I tried anyways. Every time I touched her, she moaned & spread her legs a little wider. All I wanted was some sleep, not nooky. She was half in the bag & was lying on a half eaten Eskimo Pie, melted into a brown & white puddle under her huge melons. As usual, piles of Budweiser cans were scattered all around the bed. I went down to my cot in the basement & dreamed my usual dream. I think of that dream when I sit in Pine Ridge looking for the man I am going to shoot. *In the dream purple mountains in the distant horizon are crisscrossed with lines of gray smoke from woodstoves. Inside a small, once-whitewashed shack, a fullblood woman is pulling down a parched, cracked shade. She turns on a lamp & puts on a faded shawl. Then she takes a flashlight from a drawer & walks to the small outhouse behind the shack & cries in the dark.* I wake up sweating. & I am sweating now when I think of that bastard I come here to kill.

Ten.

I think I see the buttwipe that I come down here to
do in. I leave the gas station & walk to my cousin
Jake's house in the Crazy Horse Housing Projects.
There I fit into the usual drunken, dope party. It is
getting dark outside & a light snow is falling. They
feed me but are disappointed when I refuse a hit of
coke or a can of beer. I'm just tired, I tell them &
they show me their dirty-sheet bed. Sleeping an
hour later, a man peeks into the bedroom & startles
me up. He sure looks like the one I've come for,
but he ain't. He's just another Pine Ridge drunk,
bumbling through life, from hangover to picking
beer cans. I sleep & then wake again with the
sweet mist of a forgotten sex dream & bad heartburn.
It's four in the morning & the party is over so I
walk through the living room, stepping over a dozen
passed out bodies & into the kitchen. I find some
baking soda & mix a teaspoon with a glass of water.
I burp & see a full moon of dull grade school paper
pasted against the kitchen window. I find a full
can of Coors someone has hidden & drink it slowly
& think of nothing. I walk back into the living
room & see a teenaged girl with a flat chest asleep
on the floor. I lie down next to her & fall asleep
with my lips pressed hard against her sweet, brown
Indian face.

Eleven.

A hellish scream ricochets around the house & wakes the zombie drunks. It is the howling screech of a dog hit by a car. The night of the living dead drunks shuffle to the windows & check out the world. A quick kicking German Shepherd is in the last act of the spasms of death. It shrieks like a human wounded. Everyone looks for a weapon. One finds a bat, a woman finds a mop, the girl I sleep by grabs this broom. We go out to end the misery of the four-legged. Ten drunks beat & kick the dog under the fool's full moon until blood covers shoes & snow. It quits breathing. I walk back in with the mumbling drunks & then gravity begs us to floor. The girl I've slept next to lies against me & silently undoes her blouse. In the dark stench of snoring & stinking drunks I touch her small breasts & say no words until I hear someone vomiting in a near corner. "Don't tell me your name & don't ask me mine," I tell her. She laughes a girl laugh & rustles my hair & says her name is Eileen. She's a sophomore in high school. I kiss her hand & then turn my back & I sleep hard for an hour or so until I dream of a bus bound for Hell.

Twelve.

Burping down the highway, the whale bus approaches the gates of Hell. A raspy voice grinds over the intercom: "Attention to all you hopeless skins. Anyone planning to commit murder must exit at the next stop." I look in the bag & the gun smiles back. In the seat in front of me, a man with a bad face rash that oozes yellow pus is passing out candy to children. "Tell him thanks," a dark mother warns her three children. The kids snicker & wink & the diseased man smiles timidly & walks like a spider down the aisle to the toilet at the rear of the bus. He leaves the door open & I watch him trying to scald the crud away from his reeking face with cold water. He paper towels his face & turns to face me & I see he's the one I'm going to kill but before I can move, the bus lurches into the Hell Bus Depot. I exit the bus & wait on the platform, waiting to see this enemy of mine. But as the people come off the bus, they all have disfigured faces. They are all full of bullet holes & all have much saber slashes upon their dead bodies. They are all wearing ogle wanagi, *the once sacred shirts of the Ghost Dance.*

Thirteen.

The Hell Bus Station is the life of Indians living on this stolen land. We have government food: powdered milk & powdered eggs & tin-canned horsemeat stew & powdered potatoes & cardboard steaks stained with blood red grease. Inside, the survivors of the Wounded Knee Massacre are eating maggot-hopping food. Red eyes pervade. Straight razor carrying perverts from the state pen are prowling for action among the cavalry butchered dead. In this station of the metro, tribal cops twirl bigdick batons & wear eagle feathers to cover their shame. In this dream mix of now & was I look in my bag to bring back the real. But in my bag are powdered whores, powdered winos & powdered Indian dogs. Outside a light powdered snow is falling & as I dance to the bathroom someone is singing "Jingle Bells." In the air of piss stench & cherry flavored urinal deodorants, old men are scraping whiskers with wine bottle fragments. The egg-faced man is swabbing his face in fast forward movements until it is varnished brown. Awake, I can see clearly that this man, this damn enemy, is me & that is the lie this dream thinks it tells me.

Fourteen.

We all have to go back with pain in our fat hearts to the place we grew up to grow out of. This is how we fully come to know ourselves I say to myself as I leave Jake Red Horse's house in the chilled Pine Ridge morning. In the angry earlyday sound of teens squealing tires on their way to high school, my Indian blood bubbles on the plains of my brain. I am living a lie. For twenty years I been living a lie, sedated by alcohol, unredeemed by transfusions of flesh. I go one way. My life goes another. One foot forward, one foot backward, body lurching, arms flailing, wordless, wordless, this Indian dance. I light a cigarette & stand near a cedar & contemplate the fool's mission I'm on. Vietnam wasn't this crazy. There might be more than one man here that I have ridden the bus down to kill. Maybe my plan was to do him & myself in & I'm not sure now that I will. Then again, the day is early. I scratch my head while the morning sun dances on snow-bundled children walking to school. Sometimes I'm a coward & life is ten pounds of shit in a five pound bag. And sometimes, I'm a stone-cold killer.

Part Four

CIRCLES OF FLIGHT

Crow Song

Snow is in the wind as I shovel
earth upon his welfare coffin.
In the tall, leafless cottonwoods
crows are cawing.

Thirty years ago, we stood on the soft
sand of a dirt road running
between two fields of new-mown alfalfa.
The field on the right was full of crows.
"Cawww, cawwwkkk, you eat rotten meat,"
Reno yelled and turned to his left.
In that field a lone sea gull was strutting.
Reno raised his twelve gauge and fired.
Blew the gull's head clean off.
"Hey, what's the deal?" I asked.
"Sea gulls don't belong in Nevada,"
he shrugged and walked up to the bird
and gave it a good kick.
I knew better. I knew he was pissed
at those white sailor boys from Fallon
Airbase who drove down each week
to get drunk and group-grope
his nympho sister Sandra.
I knew he was pissed at me too.
Stupid Sandra had *told* him
that she'd handjobbed me, twice!
But then she was *only* his sister
and I was his best friend.
I picked up the bloody,
white gull and punted it long,
laughing and closing the soft brown
distance in our friendship.

Now, snow is in the wind as I shovel
earth upon his welfare coffin.
In the tall, leafless cottonwoods
crows are cawing.

In the Little Waldorf Saloon at the End of the 20th Century

for Steve Gibson

The silver Thunderbird pierced and deflated the tired Nevada sun. The distant lights of Reno pulsed like a radiant whore sitting on a *bidet*, chewing gum, asking: "Was my pussy nice to you?"   On a hill above the university, there was a brief stop to stretch calcified joints, to breathe sage air, to listen to the trembling leaves of the city. Minutes later, like a drone to a queen bee, the car buzzed to a bar near the northern edge of the city. Through thirty years this bar had been in three different locations. My soul splashed down on a stool and stared at the *de rigueur* neon, the one-armed bandits and Aryan college jocks playing shuffleboard. My reflection on the tiled floor showed me serious and middle-aged and ordering a sissy nonalcohol beer. The bartender was wearing Levi's "Dockers" over cowboy boots. Bulging out of a t-shirt that said *Nevada Wolfpack,* he tapped his toes and gave me a squint. I let that go to nervousness and not man-love. This *was* Nevada. He had a tattoo that said: *Da Nang—1970,* but I was still a hard punching son of a bitch and I knew I could have stomped his ass. He moved the can from his territory to mine. I whiffed his putrid Chaps cologne and a wave of awkward, trembling sadness hit. While the ersatz dregs swilled down my throat. I gave him a five dollar tip. My homelands looked hellishly futile in sober light. Gibson, I wanted to get drunk and act young and stupid but I couldn't, just didn't have it no more.

High Plains Hailstorm

The Atlanta Braves were winning on TV
Brain-dead-looking Ted Turner and Hanoi Jane
were cameoed in their box seats
doing the "tomahawk chop."
Tens of thousands of fat Southern crackers
were whirling plastic tomahawks
when the Dakotas quickly darkened.
Outside the window drunken neighbors
were yelling and dashing with purpose.
Several squealed their *onsika* cars
under trees and threw quilts on them.
Women grabbed kids and dragged them inside.
The neighborhood had been seized
by a contagious redskin madness.
Two hawks were circling high
when sudden jerks of lightning
jumpstarted this Third World town.
The crazed electricity of Frankenstein
snapdanced through gray gravy clouds
and electrocuted an ancient cottonwood.
Hardball-sized hail came killing down.
Panic bred in our hangovers and we waited
for verminous legions of toads and snakes
to pop up from our hot toaster minds.
We closed our eyes and the storm disappeared.
In less than a minute our wondrous T-Bird
had been hammered into a total loss.
Then air was calm and the dim sun winked
On t.v. Ted and Jane were smiling
and still doing that old "tomahawk chop."

Jake and Royce

Jake's high school best pal years ago
fist-fighting a white boy yelled at his
opponent: "You ugly giggerpimp!"
The circle around the fighters hushed.
Puzzled guys nudged each other and whispered,
"What's a giggerpimp?"
The fighters were separated.
No one had the answer except Jake
and he wasn't going to spill
the beans even though he knew
that a giggerpimp was the first
cousin of a butt-whanger.
After that, they decided to get drunk
for the first time. Two tight-muscled
Indian boys sixteen years old,
Jake and his best friend Royce tossed
down two six-packs scored for them
by winos and hours later in
the broken cherry of their poisoned brains,
they sprinted up the dirt road that led to
Jake's shack, stopping halfway to gulp air.
In the full moon night a coyote yelped.
Jake let out a startled whimper and Royce
giggled. Jake punched him in the arm but
must have hit a crazy bone because Royce
howled and took a roundhouse swing
catching his friend flush on the chin.
They entered a land of shimmering red
and fell into a snarling cartoon ball of fists.
Jake ended up on top with one hand
grasping his gasping pal's throat.
The left hand of Royce came in from
outer space and hammered Jake square
on the snout. White flowers
bloomed in his young red mind.
When he came to he was forty years old
and just crawling onto the road of sobriety.
Royce died drunk in a car wreck at twenty.

Summer Solstice at Taos

*Terrible experiences make one wonder whether he
who experiences them is not something terrible.*
— Friedrich Nietzsche

Contented with stomach fire
and half-drunk, I left *La Cocina*
and maundered down backstreets
to visit an old lover from the sixties.
Why was the black tunnel of a gravel road
slightly erotic under the hairy stars?
Because ancient cottonwoods and piñon pines
lining the road had eaten the arrogance
of the dim-bulb streetlights?
I was wondering when a cat
scooted out of the darkness
and banged into my groin and scared
me so bad my balls jumped up to my throat.
Light-headed with fear, I shuddered
electrically and spit them out.
They tumbled silently onto the gravel
and gave high-pitched squeaks of hooray
before running off like quick rodents
waving their runty arms
and babbling hosannas to freedom.

Her small adobe house was crumbling
and washed in the neon blue
of a neighborhood cantina
where Valentino home boys
primped and trolled for white tourists.
She opened the door and I gasped
at her butch hair and hard, stringy body.
What role had I played in *this*?

My head spun with guilt.
I had the brief crazed fear that she
might drop her Levi's and show me
she was the new foster parent
of my runaway gonads but thank God

she didn't and thank God
I didn't have the patience to ask her
how she had turned into a man.
I could only utter, "Hello,"
and shake her hand.
A short hour later I
shook her hand again
and mumbled, "Good luck."
I was more preoccupied than troubled.
Archaic voices inside my heart
had an APB out on my absent nuts.

Dakotah Territory Hard Times

Those evil little shitbugs
got to the elms
again and ate the shade.
The dry, yellow lawn crumbled
under the panting bodies
of their aging Black Labs.
Their windows were all shut
against the choking dust
of the wheat harvesters
and the biting flies
of the nearby stockyards.
The Sears air conditioner
was sucking the life
out of their shrinking
checking account and teasing
them with sporadic wheezes of winter.
They took a cold shower together
and then walked to the drug store.
The old Indian couple loitered
near shelves of over-the-counter
sleeping pills and smiled
at their dark dreams mingling.

Blame It on the Dog, He's Dead

Waiting in the vet's office
someone's young border collie bitch
prances near our seat.
You stagger to sniff on stiff legs
and fall into a pool of shame,
whining in pain.

The imagery of innocence
lies buried in the dust.
Your body's tired mandate
won't send your dreams
to streets of lust.

Several dollars buys release
and I fake no maudlin tears.
I think of the strength
of your quick parade
down the partial path of my years.

Several dollars buys release
and I fake no maudlin tears
but an hour later, I almost wipe
the slate clean
of the chalked days
of four thirsty years.

I See an Indian Girl I Used to Know near Larimer Street in Denver

The sly goddess darkness
eye-shadowed the street.

Filled it with white cannibals
all looking for meat.

The hush of night
was on her hair.

Her tight mini-skirt
hot-riveted my stare.

She stood so poised
awaiting cars

and the lonely drift
from the closing bars

but I turned my car quickly
and sped from that place

after the bleak horror dawned
that I once knew *his* face

and still talked to *his* brothers and sisters.

Day of the Living Dead

Oh blood searing pain where the knife had been!
Last night I banished you
from my veins
but this morning you returned
with the red sun at dawn.
You brought maggot-ridden ghosts.
You brought memories of lost loves
and high school hardons.

Oh blood searing pain where the knife had been!
Sweet morphine bleached you out . . . and let
me hobble through gravel streets
overflowing with scabby-faced winos
to the Pine Ridge Post Office
to get the letter
I didn't think would be there
but was and said nothing
of consequence, except to confirm
my soul's poverty.

Sweet morphine cannot bleach that out.

Stoned to the Bone

*They must have burned like men always
burn when gasoline is poured over them.*

— Tom Page

At eleven-thirty at night Jake and
Verdell conspired to make last call.
They said the thick cobwebs
inside their brains were knitted red
with flashing pain.

Just that morning they were no-tail kites
and from wine clouds
life looked just right
but then their bottle hit empty
and the sun vanished so
they begged me to drive them
to White Clay, Nebraska.

They knew I'd bitch and moan
but they also knew I'd do it.
I told them that if I could quit
drinking then anyone could
but these damn *tahansis*
was stoned to the bone,
far gone beyond the ghosts
of our blood-soiled ways.
We walked to my car
and I mind-plugged my ears.
I refused to listen
to their deathsongs
even though for many years
those same sad sounds
squeaked past my own lips.

A Savage Blood Thirst

The morning had *taniga* breath.
Jake's lumpy bed was sweating.
The Great Plains breeze lay
red-eyed, unshaven in his yard.
The living stink of hopelessness
threw a rock though his window
and crawled in to kiss him.
Its chancred tongue licked
his soul dry and he smiled.

He staggered up to close the window
and saw a thirteen-year-old
neighbor girl singing and skipping by.
She saw him and grinned and waved.
In mad, sober light his spirit air-danced
and floated past ancient honor.
His heart, once imbedded in dust,
then cataloged for the last time
the tarantula movements
of his middle-aged lust.

He shook his head
and took three aspirins
and crawled back to bed.

Listening to Verdell

I.

"Geez, man, why in hell
do these *wasicus* make TV
programs with fake laughing?
What's the matter
with them people anyways?"

II.

"We don't know how
to talk to our women.
That's why we lose them to white men.
When Indian women hear someone
really trying to communicate with them,
they fall like spread eagles
down on the floor."

III.

"We partied like hell when I was a kid
but we never stole nothing
and never killed no one yet.
These kids today ought to be rounded up
and herded over a cliff or something
until they learn to fly right."

IV.

"One little, two little, ten little Indians.
Well, four got diabetes and dialysis.
Ennut, three caught cirrhosis and died.
Two joined the Army.
Ted Elk Boy ran from the draft in '68
and never did beam back.
I always wondered about Elk Boy.
Maybe's a priest or got AIDS or some shit."

Indian Giver

When the white man
at the Indian college
made all the instructors
sit in a circle, Indian-style,
I sat outside and thought
that if the Sacred Hoop
is truly broken, (as it was said
Black Elk said) then who
really broke the sucker?
I mean where does Black E. end
and Neihardt begin?
It's this Indian thing again
and again until we vanish
from this red soil.
Listen. Why should we respect our elders?
They got us into this mess
in the first place.
My dogs understand.
They sneak off and get flesh-fanged.
They return porcupine-quilled
and skunk-stinking but prance
like poodles when the old lady
leashes them into walks.
I try to tell her that occasionally
I need a younger woman.
I try to tell her that my veins are dry.
She just doesn't listen.
I have always given her my love.
I only want it back once in a while.
Jesus, am I asking too much?

Part Five

POSTSCRIPTS

Relapse: Blue Spring at Pine Ridge

for Jimmy Santiago Baca

I.

Things were going *too* well, Verdell said.
He had not had a drink
in three months and the glare-eyed ghosts
of warriors danced in his house, but in sober light
he thought the house seemed slightly different.
The carpet had changed from grime to almost clean
and a strange loving woman shared his bed.
Things were going *too* well. The phone rang
and some man said her name over the lines.
Tough stud Verdell said, "who-the-fuck"
and whoever was calling hung up.
At that instant, Verdell got a buzzing in his ear
and something snapped in his eye.
His tongue spasmed so he cursed his woman
and ran to his pickup.
He peeled rubber away from himself
and the long bottled dreams
of his youth came keening.

II.

Verdell called his woman a slut and lost her.
Later, bored and saddened to the point
of wiping green boogers on new blue Levis,
he supposed in rhetorical retrospective
there were other words he might have used
instead of sputtering *slut*
when his tongue blanched white
inside the vise of *angst.*

One word misused and slurred
is heard by those who can hear
as nothing more than history
repeating its ungovernable self.
He'd been sober three Jesus-thanking months,

but bleeding dusk found him speeding
through the white pine hills
to Rushville, Nebraska
and the redneck bars and liquor stores
up, up and worlds away
from the indigo intricacies
of bruised and bumbling Pine Ridge.

III.

Ghastly drunk, he ghosted home hours later
through ground blizzards swirling and hypnotic.
Said he might've blacked out for a brief, daft moment
and lost his soul at sixty miles an hour
on ice-packed roads as he buzzed
back from Rushville to Pine Ridge
through the mountains having made last
call at the cowboy bars.
Hurtling through white blindness, he saw
his skull reflected in the windshield.
He forced a smile, slowed down and lived
to beat the gaping embrace
of smashed flesh soon to freeze.

Verdell carried a filled snout and a trunk full
of poisonous nectar and was "Sittin' in ya ya,
waitin' for my la la" with Lee Dorsey on cassette
crooning as he careened homeward
cradling an Army issue .45
some drunken *tahansi* had hocked to him.
His woman was AWOL when he flopped
home to bed.

IV.

The next morning after a hot-cold shower,
aspirins, B-complex, a whiff of ammonia
and six cups of coffee, he drove away from the silence
to Martin and the LaCreek Wildlife Refuge.

Mallards circled the burned-out bulb
of the ugly fake lake.
Behind his chilled window, he put on Dorsey again
but the tape didn't do the trick.
The prismatic-necked males led
the brown females toward the chilled waters.
The earth opened up but no Orpheus returned.
Unemployed redskin shotguns married
feathers to blood to cold, cobalt earth.

Verdell reached under the seat for the .45
and saw that it had the full clip
he had bought it with.
Thank God for such small favors, he said
after he tossed it in the water
and drove his ass fast away.

V.

Weeks later, at one of the first powwows
of the season, his woman forgave him.
Spring returned like familiar sex
grown fervent and unrepentant
and the women were singing
outside the circle of singing men.
Their lilting notes lifted his eyes
to the dark night outside
the Pine Ridge *wacipi* grounds.
One-eyed cars were wheezing through dust,
squinting for parking places and were coating
the entering crowds with a thin veneer
of white clay, making them walk
the angles of angels
of death.

Wild Indians were everywhere
and still the women sang.
They mouthed the very sounds of survival
outside the circle of men singing stronger.

The whole world was held in their tawny arms
and the sweetness of brown embrace.
Those siren women softened the impending
demise of that long-dying race
until the raging drum drowned
their elkskin voices.

The drum chose not to punish Verdell
and knock him to the dust
but to strengthen his own frailties.
After the grand entry and a few honor songs, he prayed
and then trudged his sad, middle-aged body away
from the spinning dancers and frybread stands.
He started his pickup and waited for his woman.
From under the seat, he pulled out a new pint
but tossed it into a clump of spring willows.
He turned on the radio to white Gordon's KSDZ
and Hank Williams was singing *Kawliga!*
That ain't no bullshit, he told Jake later.
Said he stared hard at those willows
and grunted and groaned
until his urge to die died.

Practicing Death Songs

I was practicing death songs.
My woman left to visit her brothers
and I sat in the dark yard drinking Pepsi.
A solitary red star blinked
and a one-eyed coyote screamed
a sententious sermon from a nearby hill.
The mothering smoke from woodstoves
wended across the reservation and gathered
the ghost of a girl I loved.

That night it was hard to remember her face
because she had the most perfect
body I'd ever seen. Yes.
I confess we were stone-cold freaks
in the Haight '66 through '68.

Because of the spurned sun
of our generation
and the dope in our blood
we always stuttered our prayers of life.
We were married to the wind
and it blew the flesh from our bones.
I left her outside the Student Union
in Berkeley in December of '68.
She was screeching a folk song
like some grade-B Baez
and I was tired of the scene
so I stuck out my thumb
and headed East and lost her forever.

My loins were clean-young
and in deep need of scarring then.
She'd die of fright if she saw me now.
Small blotches of wisdom
have tainted my soul.
I accept the essential tawdriness
and tiredness of lust and
I now know that my girl dog
can bark prayers to Jesus.

But that night I sang,
I knew the weight of the shadows
had withered my soul
and soon would shatter my heart.
That was why
I was practicing death songs.

Little White Lies

One day things were just fine.
He thrashed his groin twice
before dressing for high school.
In the dusk of the stadium
that evening his strong red
blood pumped under the grey
dome of autumn.
A pretty girl in the stands smiled.
He caught two TD passes and
that night after the dance, he
first touched the bearded clam.
The next morning, he had gray
hair and false teeth.
He owned jars of pills for high
blood pressure and ulcers.
When he climbed out of bed,
the moon turned green
and trees froze and snapped.
Wild, demonic horses camped
upon his front porch
and crapped to their hearts' content.
Toads set up headquarters
beneath his couch
and took command
of his remote control.
All they wanted was MTV
and Michael Jackson's new
video: Michael, face bleached
white, nose castrated of its
African proudness.
Michael, looking like
a young Elizabeth Taylor.
Michael, sharing his mental
disorders with the world.
Michael, the anti-Christ.
Michael, America's karma
come home to roost.

Note to a Culture Vulture

May you walk swiftly into a midget with buck teeth.
— Scarecrow

Some years ago
in your infinite European boredom
you finally concluded
that maybe Indians *are* really
a noble race, yes, somewhat tragic
but definitely tied to the earth.
So, you decided to become one.
Why not? Who would care?
And who would know the difference?
Your cheekbones *were* a little high
and you *were* a little dark.
Besides, everyone has an Indian passed out
in the rotting branches of their family tree.

Days sneaked into years while feathers
took root in your brain
and burst through your skull
to air-dance dry.
With your beaded words
and researched knowledge you became
well-known as a *Native American* writer.
I envied your university job
and I used to say that you were just
another fucking white thief
stealing what little we have left
but I just bought your new book
and I liked it, a little.

That Great Wingless Bird

for Fred Whitehead

On the couch I was thrashing
and trying to meditate with my dogs
sprawled across the worn linoleum
when the automatic shots rang out.
First, I thought it was a car backfiring
on the street or the neighbor kids
getting an early start on the 4th of July
but it was only bad actors on the television
running amok, shooting up a prop world with Uzzis.
Relieved and then bored by this violent movie
on a cable channel, I dozed dreaming
of some dope-infested, gang-fighting
third or last world where women were screaming.
The pop-pop-poppa of small arms fire tingled
my ears once more and I think I awoke
to ear-reaming cop sirens.
Disgusted with violence, I shut off the tube
and dry-humped the couch.
Twinkling stars danced lewdly
outside my cheap curtained windows.

In the morning when I let my dogs out,
they ran to the hard clay driveway
I share with welfare neighbors
and danced in a pool of slow syrup blood.
When they began to lick it, I ran
after them, picked up some empty
shell casings and threw them
at their crazy asses. Vampire dogs!
Later that morning I answered a letter
from a university professor
(who claimed to be Cherokee) a world away
from this land of dead eagles and wild dogs.

"Dear Madame: (I began)

In answer to your query regarding

changing cultural patterns among
the indigeous Amerinds of the Great Plains,
well, here be what it is:

Our now culture is a nuthouse shell
covering varied worlds of denial.
Sometimes, we strip buck naked
and superglue chicken feathers to our butts
and prance around in circles.
We tell each other this is what our elders wanted.
What they wanted to preserve
before they exited their own generations
having failed at most things
except the ability
to procreate.

However, yes, we can and will
still do this prairie chicken, butt-shaking
traditional hoedown whenever we get the urge
but first we must each eat an Indian taco.
Then, we get in a circle and hop,
propelled by taco gas and prize money.
Later, we hock our commods
and let our kids go wild and hungry
as we drink, bingo, and drive endlessly
looking for hints of feathered warriors
and hoping for beauty,
that great empty word.

Yes, hoping for beauty,
that great wingless bird."

Burial Detail

In the winter air
the sounds were strange
and almost immutable.
Anyway you sliced them,
they were maudlin.

The silly staccato
of sh-sh-sh-sh
could have been
machine gun sounds
aimed in childhood
at rows of olive
green plastic soldiers
but Verdell quickly renounced
that quirky thought.
It was, nevertheless
a sound of children
the sh-sh-sh-sh-sh
the calming, the silencing, the only sounds
his middle-aged mouth
could make to his girlfriend
when she wept
while he dug
their dog's grave.

Getting Ready to Go Cold Turkey

I.

One December stoned winter day
four years ago ice eagles with razor beaks
circled my houseplants
disdaining my once-firm flesh.
They said they were staying until August.

II.

April. The house was filled with all
species of birds and they said
they were there for revenge.
That on the searing sand of Paiute land
I blew blackbirds from blue sky
for no reason but blood.
Christ, I told them. I was only a kid.
We all did that kind of crap
back then back there.

III.

June. In the circularity of karma,
the hungry bullets of youth returned
disguised as hummingbirds.
They stuck their long beaks into my eyes
and drained the nectar of sight.
I smelled the blue warmth of grave flowers.

IV.

August. I was kissing vultures by then.
Their lovely pecking opened my veins
and my mouth was full of feathers.
Nothing mattered but that lovely flight
and the ground which was light
years away.

Questions While Smoking the Pipe

In memory of Tom McGrath (1916-1990)

Late October.
Old Lakota called this month
"The moon when the wind
shakes off the leaves."
Can Wapeksna Wi.
Red willow tobacco curled from the red stone pipe.
I offered the smoke to the sacred
four directions and prayed for life
sustaining answers.

I.

Grandfather. That icicle dropped near
the front door of this HUD house.
Could it be Oedipus Complex,
that winter splinter stabbing
snow sorry he fell from the vine
or is it just another randomly stupid
dribbling of God?

II.

Grandfather.
Jake says it's better to have a hundred kids
die from gut-rotting disease
than to have Jerry Lewis bawling
and rubbing his greasy hair
against the television screens
of this Indian reservation. Is it?

III.

Grandfather.
Whatever happened to my cuz______________?
Did he ever forgive me that night
I was crashing at his apt. and I passed
out on his couch, naked with the remnants
of a bucket of the Colonel's chicken

strewn on my chest so that I
looked like some voodoo burial scene
when he brought his new black girlfriend
home for a cocktail
and later that night when I stumbled
through his bedroom to the toilet
and sat on the throne with the door open
until my gaseous explosions
startled his girl from sleep
and all I could do was smile,
give her the black power salute
and shut the door?

IV.

Grandfather. About these priests
from Holy Rosary Mission
roaming the rez with their tales.
Okay . . . Let me get this straight. God,
they say, got Mary pregnant and she had Jesus
and then Jesus died. Then Jesus became God?
Jake says if Jesus became God and God
got the cherry of the Virgin Mary
then we're talking some spooky incest here.
And just who the hell is that Holy Ghost guy?

V.

Grandfather. The Oglala Nation Fair
has the whole town walking lopsided.
Milking contempt to secure an ally,
I found some braided sweetgrass
in my underwear drawer and lit it.
Can you smell it? Can you hear them singing
49s and practicing Crow hops
down at the powwow grounds by the creek?
Listen, Grandfather!
Can you hear that drum?
Pretty damn good, *ennut*?

VI.

Grandfather, in what orbit spins Tom McGrath?
And how did it end for him?
Was it fire or ice? And for me? A coronary?
A stray bullet? Dandruff of the brain
or low grade fame?
Whatever, I'm ready whenever you call
but don't call me this year or the next,
or the damn nexteen next,
and I'll work for my people,
I promise.

The Great American Fly Novel

In his first draft, the sticking fly kicking in a high-corner web decides its impending demise is less declension of vision than rape by uncharted winds. In the diamond of its holy time, where once it winged from maggot white, it loops the loop no more, unless, well, okay, yes . . .

His computer's got him figured for a verbal and degenerate whore who can simply and seductively rewrite any score. Computer says, "Don't pout. It's not strike three. You're not out. The game's only starting."

What the computer means is why die with less than magnificent closure when you can invoke *tabula rasa* and let your dull fingers free the filthy fly into redskin autumn. So, he allows the fly to buzz through concentric circles of time, raking all doubts through a wake of wing-blurred air to a room that requires no hint of truth.

In a couple years an Indian woman lying on a bed in a reservation shack reads his novel. The first chapter shows her a gray day lunch stretched by weak martinis. The main characters are the sun-bleached matrons of a western cowturd town. All these white folks stall vitamin death and its accompanying dustwords by eating roast beef grown on land legally stolen from Indians. The sweet redflesh melts like the butter of dreams and a fat fly sky-dances above their plates. One of the matrons squishes the fly and the novel thus ends in mid-air. "I don't get it," the Indian woman says. "I thought you said your book was about Indians? Where's the Indians? Where the hell are they?"

A Rudimentary Lesson in American Indian Journalism

In memory of Alvin Fast Wolf

It was a bitter moonless night
in that time of year some Lakota call
"Moon of the Popping Trees."
At thirty-five below the dogs
were kicked out the front door.
They steam-streamed the frozen lawn
and whined violently to be let back in.
The air was so dry we boiled
water to breathe hints of summer.

At thirty-five below I left my beloved
couch and entered the distant bedroom
of my distant woman.
The cats and dogs surrounding her bed
glared momentarily and then welcomed
an source of additional heat.
Back to back we formed an ancient butterfly
encased in ice but slowly melting.
Joined at the spine, in foetal positions
we breathed quietly in desperate hope.
I knew we are both praying for sleep
but the gods were not listening.
In the automatic ritual of release
our hands went about their business
until they took recess and dangled
cigarettes in the dark.

Later, when she began to snore, I rose
to hear millions of whispering
snowflakes forming burial mounds
over our unstartable cars.
I mixed a huge seven and seven
and descended to the basement
to write a news story due that morning.
Immediately dyslexic, I got progressively worse

until the fumes of Liquid Paper
fomented the Muses
to rebel from unconsciousness.
Groggy and stung silly
by the cold, they stammered
and glared and spat with alacrity,
the famous five Ws.

Who?

Holy Mary, Mother of God,
we are the descendants of Oriental Eskimos
who carried sushi and wore
ribbon shirts and Foster Grants
when they crossed the land bridge
over the Bering Strait
on their way down to Haskell Indian School.

Where?

Hey, open your eyes
and smell the frybread!
Look for us in Bell Gardens, Schurz,
Porcupine and Potato Creek, Ethete and Dulce,
Wellpinit and Shiprock.
(We are the oldest kids on the block!)
Look in Red Lake, Blue Lake, Pyramid Lake,
on the playing fields of Cleveland,
on the silver screen with Kevin Costner.
We're always galloping through Gallup.

When?

 Anytime you feel froggy.

What?

Chicken butt, that's what.
Ask me again and I'd tell you the same.

Why?

It's simply because we're so noble.
Oh Jesus, we *are* noble red men.

The Boys Cruise Seattle

Ennut!
Look, Jake,
says Verdell.
Isn't that
Christ
on that
totem pole?
Not the one on top. That one there, squished
between the thunderbird and the bear near the
bottom.
The one that's
frowning
like someone
watching wine-stink
cousins coming
to a wake
just to eat.
Can you see
his hands?
Pull over. Let's
check them out
for nail holes.

Fish Fry at a Panhandle Bar

Grime and wheat chaff caked their skin
but these combiners reeked strongly of fish.
"We found her in the fields," one said
and sprung for a round for the house.
"First, we thought she was a drunk Indian
but Indians don't never bathe."

The rednecks began to outnumber the Indians.
Crowds of townspeople entered the bar
to stare at its newest citizen:
a sleek green mermaid with emerald nipples.
"But there ain't no ocean near Nebraska,"
one said between shots of tequila.
He even offered a shot to the mermaid.
She ignored him and eyeballed Jake and Verdell.
Flushed wide, her ancient pupils hushed
the tumescent sunset like taps
played on an alto sax.
It was not music that guided her crimson
trickling beyond blue lips.
Blood shot straight from the siren's heart
and was not mere illusion
like the Texas longhorns upon the walls.
Yards long and polished, the horns pointed
towards decades of insatiable American dreams.
The horns scaled her solitude and sharpened
the lonesome moans from those two Indian fools.
Then, clamorous dust consumed all sound.
A quaint white mob approached:
old sunbaked women with knives and linen.
One carried a bowlful of lemons. The boys
made no words to fend off white blood thirst.
Their mouths were too busy drooling.

Graffiti Dialogue in a Nebraska Bordertown Laundramat

"Chester Crow suckes a peache.
and he injoys it to."

*

"He's a lie. Indian men don't do that."

*

"He wrote himself he's bragging.
We know Chester is queer."

*

"Try me and find out you liar."

*

"Indians are ignorent! Prairie niggers move
back to Pine Ridge and eat dogs."

*

"Well screw you white trashes."

*

"C. Crow suckes a white peache to."

White Bread Blues

This day I love you because
only an Indian woman could
understand how an Indian boy
could fall in with a pack
of white bordertown kids
and allow shame to be born.
Even before we met
you knew about my childhood
family trips to town.
Mom got groceries only
after the whole family waited
for the old man to be
burped out of the bars
where he spent his fair share
of our food money
on his jealous medication.

Once in '57
when I was eleven
we were at the curb
in the town park
in our battered Chevy
pickup loaded with paper
sacks and kids eating
thick bologna sandwiches
without the miracle
of Miracle Whip.

Mom climbed out of the cab
and filled a glass gallon jar
at the water fountain
by the court house.
Mom was unashamed
to mix Kool-Aid
in public but when my white
friends with smiling eyes
rode by on their new bicycles
I put on an Indian face

and pretended not to see them.
I prayed one day I'd live a life
as white as store-bought bread
where dark lives did not exist
but my prayer was never
answered, thank God.

No, no, no, not God.
Thank you, Grandfather.
Thank you, Grandfather.

Buffalo Spirit Song

for Robert Gay, 1946-1993

Great God
of any particular mood.
Sometimes it is all
too bovinely obvious.
Driving home from the Indian college
I followed a car jammed full
of buffalo heads snaking
along the road to White Clay.

Belching smoke on a blistering day
the rusted heap of a car cruised,
exuding the miasma of red
men with holes in their souls
and not one thin dime
for a bottle of ease.
It is a picture I have recorded
a thousand times and more.
There is nothing new here
except an invisible change in philosophy.
I used to think that if real men
did exist, then they existed on the wires
of that eternal magnetism
between cock and cunt.
I now know that real men
do not exist and never have.
I speak as a member
of a herd of mammals
who can dance and cry
words on paper.

Between Blue Earth

Between Blue Earth
and Rochester, MN
I counted thirteen coons
deflated, smashed and oozing
and one dead badger, inflated
into a gaseous oval
like all I had to do
was tie a string around its big toe
and I could balloon skyward
far away from my foolish quest
of interviewing for a job in Rochester.
Christ on a paper crutch. Cruising
through town I saw no dark faces.
Rochester, MN was nothing
more than the antiseptic waiting
room of the Mayo Clinic
Ten minutes after I got there
I went to KFC and called the school
and said "I ain't taking your job, I've
got me a serious illness."
Officially unemployed, I ordered
some barbecued wings
with my dwindling funds.
Another safari completed, I turned around
and ate the chicken wings as I
headed back towards Pine Ridge.
640 miles to darkness.

Cherry Tomato

You rubbed the cherry tomato
on your jeans and then plopped
it into my mouth.

My dentures released the wild scent
of something we almost did together.
We did dig the garden by hand.
Shoveled this Dakota clay
until it became hospitable
for the mums and pansies
we bought at Safeway over in
Chadron, but after four weeks
they were murdered
by the cherry tomatoes
that come back
yearly to choke
our flowers.

We were back together again
after my brief fling
with a younger woman.
You kissed me on the cheek
and then shoved another
red globe down my gullet.
You told me I was too old
to be chasing young girls
and I nodded like I thought
you were right but down
below old one-eyed Joe
was winking.

Notes on the Text

"A Postcard from Devils Tower"—*Hanbleceya* is Lakota term for a vision quest in which a person fasts for three days on a hill and prays for a guiding vision or communication with the spirits and/or the Creator. It is a type of ludicrous irony to suggest that Crazy Horse worked for white ranchers. Devils Tower, written about most notably by Scott Momaday, is near Sundance, Wyoming, approximately two hours north of Rapid City, South Dakota.

"Sifting The Ashes of Greek Fire"— The term "forty-nine" is a Pan-Indian term used to describe a type of song, and a type of celebration, usually involved with singing and sometimes drinking after a pow-wow, since liquor is not allowed at powwows.

"For My Lakota Woman"— *Unci* is Lakota for "grand-mother." The Centennial of the Wounded Knee Massacre was observed in December of 1990.

"Verdell: Two Soliloquies"— *Kola* is Lakota for "friend." *Wacipi* and *wasicu* are Lakota terms for "dance" (Indian powwow dancing) and "white man," respectively. *Ennut* is a western Indian affirmation meaning (at various times) "yes," "okay," "that's so," etc. Sometimes spelled *ennit* or *enit*.

"A Brand New Snag"—"Snag" is a term used by many western Indians to denote a date, a pickup, or one's opposite in a longer relationship.

"The Blood Thirst of Verdell Ten Bears" (Part Six) — *dona* (Lakota) for "many." The term "Green Lizard" is used to describe pints of Gibson's Musca-tel wine, the preferred poison on many reservations. (Part Seven) — *Tahansi* (Lakota) for "cousin" in direct familial sense and in the larger sense of being fellow tribal members. (Part Twelve) — The reference to "shirts of the Ghost Dance" is intended to be ironic. The *ogle wanagi*, the ghosts shirts, were thought by some Lakota to be impervious to bullets.

"High Plains Hailstorm" — There has been a recent and increasing controversy over the use of Indian-related names for team names and mascots. The use of the "tomahawk chop" by the Atlanta Braves baseball team has particularly incensed many Indian people. Furthermore, many feel the use of such team names as "Braves," "Chiefs," "Indians," and "Redskins" shows an intolerable insensitivity towards the original inhabitants of this country. *Onsika* is Lakota for "pitiful."

"Summer Solstice at Taos" — APB is short for "all-points bulletin."

"A Savage Blood Thirst" — *Taniga* (Lakota) for "tripe" or "tripe soup." *Taniga* soup is a traditional dish that one has to acquire a taste for. Some people find it too pungent.

"That Great Wingless Bird" — "commods" is the shortened form of "commodities," the USDA surplus food that is the staple of so many reservation diets.

About the Author

Born and raised in northern Nevada, Adrian C. Louis is the eldest of twelve children. A mixed-blood Indian, he is an enrolled member of the Lovelock Paiute Tribe and is a graduate of Brown University, where he also earned an M.A. in Creative Writing.

Since 1984 he has taught English at Oglala Lakota College on the Pine Ridge Reservation of South Dakota. Prior to this, Adrian Louis has been the editor of four tribal newspapers, including a stint as Managing Editor of the *Lakota Times,* America's largest Indian newspaper. He was twice nominated as Print Journalist of the Year by the National Indian Media Consortium, and he was a co-founder of the Native American Press Association.

The poems of Adrian Louis have been widely anthologized, and his collection **Fire Water World** (West End Press: 1989) won the Book Award from San Francisco State University. **Among the Dog Eaters**, also from West End Press, was published in 1992. A new collection of his poems, **Vortex of Indian Fevers**, has recently been accepted for publication in 1995.

Adrian Louis has won fellowships from the Wurlitzer Foundation, the South Dakota Council on the Arts, the Bush Foundation, the National Endowment for the Arts, and the Nebraska Arts Council. His first novel, **Skins**, has been accepted for publication, and he is currently working on a second novel.

Also available from **Time Being Books**®

LOUIS DANIEL BRODSKY
You Can't Go Back, Exactly
The Thorough Earth
Four and Twenty Blackbirds Soaring
Mississippi Vistas: Volume One of *A Mississippi Trilogy*
Falling from Heaven: Holocaust Poems of a Jew and a Gentile
   (with William Heyen)
Forever, for Now: Poems for a Later Love
Mistress Mississippi: Volume Three of *A Mississippi Trilogy*
A Gleam in the Eye: Poems for a First Baby
Gestapo Crows: Holocaust Poems
The Capital Café: Poems of Redneck, U.S.A.

HARRY JAMES CARGAS (editor)
Telling the Tale: A Tribute to Elie Wiesel on the Occasion of His
   65th Birthday — Essays, Reflections, and Poems

ROBERT HAMBLIN
From the Ground Up: Poems of One Southerner's Passage to Adulthood

WILLIAM HEYEN
Falling from Heaven: Holocaust Poems of a Jew and a Gentile
   (with Louis Daniel Brodsky)
Erika: Poems of the Holocaust
Pterodactyl Rose: Poems of Ecology
Ribbons: The Gulf War — A Poem
The Host: Selected Poems 1965-1990

TED HIRSCHFIELD
German Requiem: Poems of the War and the Atonement of a Third
   Reich Child

VIRGINIA V. JAMES HLAVSA
Waking October Leaves: Reanimations by a Small-Town Girl

RODGER KAMENETZ
The Missing Jew: New and Selected Poems

NORBERT KRAPF
Somewhere in Southern Indiana: Poems of Midwestern Origins

JOSEPH MEREDITH
Hunter's Moon: Poems from Boyhood to Manhood

FOR OUR FREE CATALOG OR TO ORDER

(800) 331-6605
Monday through Friday, 8 a.m. to 4 p.m. Central time
FAX: (314) 432-7939